PROSPERITY:

The Choice Is Yours

KENNETH COPELAND

KENNETH

COPELAND

PUBLICATIONS

Unless otherwise noted, all scripture is from the *King James Version* of the Bible.

Scripture quotations marked *The Amplified Bible* are from *The Amplified Bible, Old Testament* © 1965, 1987 by The Zondervan Corporation. *The Amplified New Testament* © 1958, 1987 by The Lockman Foundation. Used by permission.

Scripture quotations marked *New International Version* are from *The Holy Bible, New International Version* © 1973, 1978, 1984 by the International Bible Society. Used by permission of Zondervan Publishing House.

Prosperity: The Choice Is Yours
ISBN-10: 0-88114-728-1   30-0027
ISBN-13: 978-0-88114-728-5

12 11 10 09 08   16 15 14 13 12

© 1985 Eagle Mountain International Church Inc. aka Kenneth Copeland Ministries

Kenneth Copeland Publications
Fort Worth, TX 76192-0001

For more information about Kenneth Copeland Ministries, call 800-600-7395 or visit www.kcm.org.

Contents

Introduction

I am excited about *Prosperity: The Choice Is Yours* because it has been birthed by a natural flow of revelation knowledge from my heart to yours. If you are experiencing financial trouble, this book is for you.

I desire with all my heart that you prosper and be in health, even as your soul prospers. (See 3 John 2.) I pray that, as you read the following pages, you will be inspired to reach out beyond yourself in giving to the needs of others and receive revelation from the Holy Spirit—His wisdom and direction for your personal prosperity, in the Name of Jesus.

Kenneth Copeland

1

The Whole Gospel

In our effort to proclaim the gospel of Jesus Christ, is there a portion that we have forgotten? Is there a part we left out? What is the whole gospel? Let's look at the Gospel of Luke and find out.

And he [Jesus] came to Nazareth, where he had been brought up: and, as his custom was, he went into the synagogue on the sabbath day, and stood up for to read. And there was delivered unto him the book of the prophet Esaias [or, Isaiah]. And when he had opened the book, he found the place where it was written, The Spirit of the Lord is upon me, because he hath anointed me to preach the gospel to the poor; he hath sent me to heal the brokenhearted, to preach deliverance to the captives, and recovering of sight to the blind, to set at liberty them that are bruised, to preach the acceptable year of the Lord. And he closed the book, and he gave it again to the minister, and sat down. And the eyes of all them that were in the synagogue were fastened on him. And he began to say unto them, This day is this scripture fulfilled in your ears (Luke 4:16-21).

I want you to notice that Jesus did not simply make the statement, "This day is this scripture fulfilled in your ears." It says, "He *began* to say unto them." Verses 18-19 are a summary of what He said. I believe they are a short outline of a sermon that He was about to preach. Verse 22 says, "And all bare him witness, and wondered at the gracious words which proceeded out of his mouth…." Obviously, He continued to speak.

In the light of this scripture, the gospel has never been preached to the poor. I'm not talking about the new birth. I'm talking about each of the categories that Jesus mentioned in these scriptures.

He was anointed to preach. To the captives,

He preached deliverance. To the brokenhearted, He preached healing. To the blind, He preached recovery of sight. He outlined here that the gospel covers many areas. We have preached healing, recovering of sight, deliverance and the new birth to the poor; but we have never preached *the gospel* to the poor.

The Gospel to the Poor

What is the gospel to the poor? The gospel to the poor is that Jesus has come and they don't have to be poor anymore! Not very many poverty-stricken people have ever heard the whole gospel. Most of them have heard that they are supposed to live a meager existence. That is what the missionaries who preached to them believed!

When I was in Africa, the Lord told me that He is holding the Body of Christ in every nation responsible for winning their own lost. It takes money to finance a revival. How can they believe for any prosperity in Africa or India, where drought and famine have become a way of life? That is a major part of my calling. I'm responsible for teaching the nations to observe to do all Jesus commanded.

There are always some missionaries who will become upset and argue, "You can preach abundance in the United States, but don't come to Africa and preach it." Or, they tell me, "It won't work in El Salvador." "It won't work in Nicaragua," etc.

But when you are preaching the Word of God, it works. God could care less whether anyone listening has a dime or not. He didn't base His gospel on what government happens to be in power at the time. All God is looking for is faith! There is enough undiscovered wealth in the poorest nations to turn their poverty into abundance if they would just believe the gospel. Even if there weren't, God is more than able to put it there.

The Kingdom of God Produces "Things"

Abundance and prosperity are important to the kingdom of God. Jesus said that if you seek first the kingdom of God and His righteousness, all these *things* will be added to you. (See Matthew 6:33.) You can't tell me that the kingdom of God is not connected to abundance. If it were not, then things would not be produced when you seek His kingdom.

The Bible says, "Every matter may be established by the testimony of two or three witnesses" (Matthew 18:16, *New International Version*). The second witness to the thought that the gospel has not been preached to the poor, is Luke 7:20-22:

> When the men were come unto him
> [Jesus], they said, John Baptist hath sent
> us unto thee, saying, Art thou he that
> should come? or look we for another?
> And in that same hour he cured many of
> their infirmities and plagues, and of evil
> spirits; and unto many that were blind he
> gave sight. Then Jesus answering said unto
> them, Go your way, and tell John what
> things ye have seen and heard; how that
> the blind see, the lame walk, the lepers
> are cleansed, the deaf hear, the dead are
> raised, to the poor the gospel is preached.

Jesus listed very specific categories. One of them was preaching the good news to the poor man, thereby giving him hope and strength.

We need to stop allowing these poverty-stricken people to believe that staying poor will somehow make them more pious and sanctified. If this were true, the people of today's starving Third World nations would be holy right now!

Poverty is an evil spirit. I remember one of my junior-high-school teachers telling my mother something that has marked my thinking all these years. He said, "I was raised in deep poverty. I fought my way through high school and through a college degree to get away from it." But he said, "I don't care how hard I try and how hard I work, I still smell that poverty. I can't get away from it."

I remember thinking, *I wonder why he still smells poverty?* It was because the spirit of poverty was still with him. Many rich people are operating under this spirit. It drove them to become rich. If the spirit of poverty can compel a man to become wealthy, it will drive him to keep his wealth as well. You would think a person who was raised in poverty would be motivated to get others out of it. But they won't turn loose of what they have. They are afraid they will lose it and end up poor again. That same spirit of poverty is still dominating them today, even though they are wealthy.

Three Things We Must Know

The Body of Christ must know three things regarding the laws of prosperity. If you are ignorant of them, whether you're rich or poor, you are a problem going somewhere to happen.

1. You must know that it is God's will to prosper His people. God is not limited by what part of the world you live in or what government you live under. Believers all over the world have proven this fact. I've heard testimonies of God prospering people in the most devastated places like Africa, El Salvador, Nicaragua and South America. The laws that govern abundance work for anyone who will put them to work. They are *laws!*

People have the idea that spiritual things are separate from material things. That isn't true. Spiritual laws govern material things. A Spirit created all matter. So the laws of prosperity will work for anyone who will meet the biblical requirements to walk in them.

2. You need to know God's reason for prospering His people. The Word says, "Let him that stole steal no more: but rather let him labour, working with his hands the thing which is good, that he may have to give to him that needeth" (Ephesians 4:28).

The whole purpose for gainful employment and prosperity is to take God's laws and prosper by them, and then do something about the poverty in the rest of the world.

Some rich people don't want to do anything but stay rich. But if I reach out and preach the gospel to a born-again man from Mozambique, he has some hope for the first time in his life. He learns that God wants to prosper him and his people. To the starving man that doesn't mean a Cadillac! It means that God will show him how to get some rain on his scorched ground. God will do something about the poisons in his land, so he can grow good crops and feed his family.

The gospel not only gives him hope in the kingdom to come, but through Jesus, and the message that God wants to prosper His people, it gives him hope in the here and now! God intended for material creation to bless and prosper His people.

3. The last thing we must know is God's way of prospering His people. God prospers first by prospering the soul (3 John 2) and through the avenue of giving. We can't solve the world's problems with our natural, limited minds, but if we'll allow God to illuminate our human consciousness with His way of thinking, nothing is impossible.

God wants to elevate our thinking to His level. He wants to prosper our souls with the answer. Begin by giving financially. A giving attitude will begin to take over and then turn into a giving lifestyle. This attitude should take over the entire Body of Christ.

God Is Shaking the World's Wealth

The wealth of the earth belongs to God. Haggai 2:7-9 says: "And I will shake all nations, and the desire of all nations shall come: and I will fill this house with glory, saith the Lord of hosts. The silver is mine, and the gold is mine, saith the Lord of hosts. The glory of this latter house shall be greater than of the former…."

God is shaking this world's system. The wealth that the world has accumulated is going to fall out of their hands. Into whose hands will it fall? Proverbs 28:8 says, "He that by usury and unjust gain increaseth his substance, he shall gather it for him that will pity the poor."

This is why God keeps telling the Church to

do something about the poor. We have let the government handle our responsibility. They have put patches on the problem instead of solving it. If the Church of Jesus Christ would get involved by sharing the new birth and preaching the gospel to the poor, poverty could be broken instead of multiplied.

Forget your own needs. Get involved in the whole gospel. Begin to meet the needs of others, spirit, soul and body, and watch how quickly God will move in your behalf. Remember what we read earlier from the words of Jesus in Matthew 6:33, "Seek ye first the kingdom…and all these things shall be added unto you." One of the great keys to this is to take your eyes off of your own life and put them on the lives and needs of others.

2

The Source of Prosperity

Beloved, I wish above all things that thou mayest prosper and be in health, even as thy soul prospereth. For I rejoiced greatly, when the brethren came and testified of the truth that is in thee, even as thou walkest in the truth. I have no greater joy than to hear that my children walk in truth (3 John 2-4).

The man who wrote these verses was no novice to spiritual things. He lived night and day with Jesus. He walked and talked with the Master. In his later years, he received insights from the Spirit of God into future generations and penned the book of Revelation. His name was John, the apostle of love.

While reading these verses written by this man who knew Jesus so well, I came across the words "I wish," or better translated, "I pray," and it caught my attention. I want to know anything that one of the apostles would pray. And if Jesus thought enough of John to place His own mother in his care, I want to know what this man has to say!

The apostle writes, "Beloved, I [pray] above all things that thou mayest prosper and be in health, even as thy soul prospereth. For I rejoiced greatly, when the brethren came and testified of the truth that is in thee, even as thou *walkest in the truth*."

Here John connects "walking in the truth" (the Word) with the ability to prosper and be in health. Healing and prosperity then, must be direct products of being filled with and walking in the Word of God.

The Word says that if you seek first the kingdom of God and His righteousness, things will be added to you (Matthew 6:33). In seeking first the kingdom of God, you *must first seek the Word, learn to walk in the Word and get the Word inside you.* Then things will be added to you. If you walk daily in His Word and in His truth, you have a sure connection to health and prosperity.

Take Hope

After giving his long life to the service of Jesus Christ, an aging Apostle John "rejoiced greatly" when he heard that "my children walk in truth." I, too, can take hope in his joy because I know, like John, that if I walk in the Word I can rejoice in the knowledge that God is greater than any situation anywhere, anytime.

It doesn't matter how high interest rates become. That's not going to defeat me, and it's not going to defeat the Body of Christ. We have hope. We are going to be healthy—people for the world to look up to. And when they ask, "Where are you getting it?" we can look at them with a smile and say, "Our God meets all our needs according to His riches in glory." Praise the Lord!

Psalm 35:27-28 says, "Let them shout for joy, and be glad, that favour my righteous cause: yea, let them say continually, Let the Lord be magnified, which hath pleasure in the prosperity of his servant. And my tongue shall speak of thy righteousness and of thy praise all the day long."

Doesn't that thrill you? You can take hope in this scripture. God has pleasure in your prosperity. He takes pleasure in your healing. God is pleased when you prosper in every area of your life.

The Word says, "Let them say [it] continually, Let the Lord be magnified…. And my tongue shall speak of thy righteousness and of thy praise all the day long"! This means continually, steadily walking in His Word. It means meditating on God and His promises "all the day long." If you do this day after day, God's Word will eventually take root in your soul. When your soul starts to walk continually in His truth, God's blessings are not far off. You will prosper even as your soul prospers.

Joshua was a good example of a man who continually walked in the Word. He meditated on and took hope in God's promise of a land that flowed with milk and honey. He held to the promise and eventually became the leader of the Israelites after Moses died.

Moses was a tough act to follow, but in Joshua 1:5, God assured, "There shall not any man be able to stand before thee all the days of thy life: as I was with Moses, so I will be with thee: I will not fail thee, nor forsake thee."

If I had my name written at the top of this verse and God said to me, "[Kenneth], there shall not any man be able to stand before thee all the days of thy life: as I was with Moses, so I will be with thee. I will not fail thee nor forsake thee," I could take hope in that! That promise can be just as strong to me today as it was to Joshua back then, if I meditate in the Word night and day.

God went on to tell Joshua in verses 7-8, "Only be thou strong and very courageous, that thou mayest observe [understand] to do according to all the law, which Moses my servant commanded thee: turn not from it to the right hand or to the left, *that thou mayest prosper withersoever thou goest.* This book of the law shall not depart out of thy mouth; *but thou shalt meditate therein day and night….*"

Some people say, "Well, I don't have that much time, Lord. I've only got 15 minutes a day." If that's all the time you've got, that's all the result you will get! Jesus said, the way you measure it, it will be measured back to you. (See Luke 6:38.)

Joshua was told to walk and meditate in the Word, and he would prosper everywhere he went. So, as you meditate in the Word continually, you will prosper. And if your soul has to prosper before you can prosper, then meditating in the Word must prosper your soul. Why is this so important?

God would rather reveal things to you that will cause your soul to prosper because a prosperous soul can hear the voice of God and be sensitive to His leading. He can then reach in and work through you to change circumstances and bring about blessings.

Jesus Is the Teacher

Let's discover the source of our prosperity. Isaiah 48:17 says, "Thus saith the Lord, thy Redeemer, the Holy One of Israel; I am the Lord thy God which teacheth thee to profit, which leadeth thee by the way that thou shouldest go." This scripture is talking about Jesus. *He is the One who prospers the soul.* No one else can do it. Jesus is the One who says, "I'll teach you how to profit!" He does it through the Word. Jesus *is* the Word.

A good example is the nation of Mozambique, at one time, one of the most devastated countries in Africa. You couldn't buy anything in that country. All the stores were closed. There was only one thing in that entire nation still alive and full of hope and faith—a strong Word-preaching church that walked in the laws of prosperity and health.

The government came to the pastor and said,

"Whatever you are doing, keep doing it. We don't care if you *do* preach Jesus. You are the only thing that's giving our people hope."

The pastor testified, "I learned about the laws of prosperity. God has taught me and prospered me all the way through this holocaust." His church is still flourishing today.

Jesus will teach *you* how to prosper. I don't care who you are, or where you are. He will teach you how to be well—spirit, soul and body—regardless of your circumstances. He said, "I am the way, the truth and the life" (John 14:6). Start walking daily in His ways. Begin meditating daily in His truth. Then His life, health and prosperity will be yours.

Prosperity—More Than Money

Through our traditional ideas, we have been led to believe that prosperity is ungodly. However, inspired by the Holy Spirit, John writes that we should prosper and be in health. Then he says in 3 John 11, "Beloved, follow not that which is evil, but that which is good. He that doeth good is of God: but he that doeth evil hath not seen God."

If prosperity is evil, why would He want us to prosper? You see, there is nothing wrong with prosperity in itself.

Money is not the root of all evil. "The *love* of money is the root of all evil" (1 Timothy 6:10), and there are people committing this sin who don't have a dime! I want you to realize, however, that prosperity covers much more than finances.

When John said we should prosper and be in health, he added the phrase, "even as thy soul prospereth." Man is a spirit. He has a soul which consists of his mind, his will and his emotions. And he lives in a body. Thus, there is spiritual prosperity, mental prosperity and physical prosperity.

To prosper spiritually, you must be born again. When you accept Jesus as your Savior and make Him the Lord of your life, your spirit is reborn and brought into fellowship with your heavenly Father. This puts you in position to receive from Him all that is promised in His Word.

To prosper in your soul, you must be able to control your mind, your will and your emotions. Just because you have accumulated a large amount of knowledge does not mean that your mind is prosperous. Prosperity of the mind comes when

you use the acquired information and learn to
control your mind instead of your mind controlling
you. Second Corinthians 10:5 says we are to cast
down imaginations and every high thing that exalts
itself against the knowledge of God [or against the
Word of God], and to bring into captivity every
thought to the obedience of Christ. The person
who does this has control of his mind and is in
position to prosper mentally. You cannot control
your mind completely without the Word of God
being alive and operating inside you. You must
harness your will in the same way.

Controlling Your Will

Some people say, "Lord, help my will to crum-
ble." God doesn't want a broken will that He can
dominate. He wants your will whole and in sub-
mission to His so that the two of you can work
together in unity.

When God made man, He gave him a will that
has power. It is actually a godlike will because man
has the right to choose his own eternal destiny. Man
was made in God's image and given the will to make
up his own mind. You can go to hell if you want to

and God will protect your right to go there…you don't have to, but you can. On the other hand, you can choose Jesus Christ and the Word of God and experience eternity with your heavenly Father. What a privilege! The choice is yours!

When a man's soul is prosperous, his will is in line with God's will. How can you get in line with God's will? You can't until you know what His Word says. His Word and His will are the same! An honest man can't will one thing and say another. If you are in line with the Word of God, you are in line with His will.

Governing the Emotions

Let's discuss our feelings as part of the soul. First of all, God made you an emotional being. You are created in His image, therefore He must experience emotions as well. The Scripture verifies that Jesus wept (John 11:35) and that God laughs (Psalm 2:4). Expressing feelings is certainly not wrong. To remain prosperous in our soul, however, we should not be motivated by our feelings.

The Gospels reveal that Jesus was moved with compassion. He said He only did what He saw

His Father do, so compassion is a Person—the
Father. Jesus expressed His feelings, but He was
not moved by them. He maintained control at all
times. He is our example. A prosperous soul must
keep emotions in line with the Word of God.

You will never be healthier or more prosperous
than your soul. You can be born again, even filled
with the Holy Spirit, and still not be prosperous in
your soul. For instance, an old saint of God, living
in poverty, can pray revival down on a church, get
everybody in town saved and be lying in bed sick
the whole time—if she does not believe the Word
of God for her own health!

True Prosperity

The world's definition of physical prosperity
(prosperity of the senses) includes gold, silver, financial
power, political power and social favor. The world's
definition of mental prosperity (prosperity of the soul) is
"knowing it all." Put these two ideas together and you
have a person who can use his mind to get financial
and political power. This is the world's total concept of
prosperity. You can easily see its drawbacks!

True prosperity is the ability to meet the needs

of mankind in any realm of life. Wealth and power cannot answer every need.

Money makes a lousy god! It can't buy good health or prevent sickness and disease from taking over the human body. Yes, it can go toward buying it, but the world's system of healing just isn't good enough. In the mental realm, a person can have all the facts in his head and not have the ability to use that knowledge to obtain the money or the health he needs.

What produces spiritual, mental and physical prosperity? What brings all these areas together? The Word of God. The Bible says in Hebrews 4:12 that the Word is alive, powerful and sharper than a two-edged sword. It says that it divides the soul and the spirit, the joints and the marrow, and that it is a discerner of the thoughts and intents of the heart. When you are walking in the Word of God, you will prosper and be in health. It is His will for us to be made whole—spirit, soul and body—and to be kept that way until the return of our Lord Jesus Christ (1 Thessalonians 5:23).

3

Prosperity—A Blessing or a Curse

Some people have the idea that to prosper financially is a curse. Others believe that if God were to bless them, He would do it by making them poor. I want us to determine from God's Word whether prosperity is a blessing or a curse. Once we do that, we can further establish the direction God wants us to take in the financial realm.

Our scriptural basis is Deuteronomy 30:19-20:

I call heaven and earth to record this day against you, that I have set before you life and death, blessing and cursing: therefore choose life, that both thou and thy seed may live: That thou mayest love the Lord thy God, and that thou mayest obey his voice, and that thou mayest cleave unto him: for he is thy life, and the length of thy days: that thou mayest dwell in the land which the Lord sware unto thy fathers, to Abraham, to Isaac, and to Jacob, to give them.

This promise applies to the New Testament believer because the covenant was made with Abraham *and his seed.* Galatians 3:29 tells us that if we are Christ's, we are Abraham's seed.

Notice that *we* are the ones who must choose. God will not make the decision for us. If we don't choose life, cursing will automatically come on us. It will be our fault, not God's.

The Curse of the Law

Since we must choose, we need to know if prosperity is a blessing or a curse. Deuteronomy 28:15 says, "It shall come to pass, if thou wilt not hearken unto the voice of the Lord thy God, to observe to do all his commandments and his statutes which I command thee this day; that all these curses shall come upon thee, and overtake thee." He is about to list some *curses*, not blessings.

Verses 16-17 say, "Cursed shalt thou be in the city, and cursed shalt thou be in the field. Cursed shall be thy basket and thy store." Your basket and store point directly to the area of finances, or lack of them.

Verse 18 says, "Cursed shall be the fruit of thy body, and the fruit of thy land, the increase of thy kine, and the flocks of thy sheep." Fruit is born or brought into being. Fruit is increase. This verse is talking about family increase as well as the flourishing of material assets.

To curse the increase means that there will not be any increase. Note that the purpose of the cursed increase was not to teach a spiritual lesson—it was to destroy! This chapter says that the curse comes to destroy until you perish. That's certainly no blessing.

Notice verse 20: "The Lord shall send upon thee cursing, vexation, and rebuke…." The verb tense in the original Hebrew indicates that God actually has nothing to do with sending these. These Hebrew verbs are permissive. God will *allow* these things to come. Once He has delegated authority, God cannot do anything else but permit them. Those who have dominion over the destruction and the curse are responsible for exercising that dominion.

God is not protecting us from the devil. As far as He is concerned, Satan has been defeated and the Body of Christ has been given authority over the evil one. This is true concerning finances as well. Poverty is a curse and the Bible says that we have been redeemed from it.

Let's continue with verse 31: "Thine ox shall be slain before thine eyes, and thou shalt not eat thereof: thine ass [or, in today's terms, 'thy car'] shall be violently taken away from before thy face, and shall not be restored to thee: thy sheep shall be given unto thine enemies, and thou shalt have none to rescue them." To lose everything—your job, your assets and your possessions—without any way to get them back, is a *curse*.

Verses 32-33 say, "Thy sons and thy daughters shall be given unto another people, and thine eyes shall look, and fail with longing for them all the day long: and there shall be no might in thine hand. The fruit of thy land, and all thy labours, shall a nation which thou knowest not eat up;

and thou shalt be only oppressed and crushed always." Our society is seeing glimpses of this. The news is flooded with reports of children who have been kidnapped or reported missing. Parents are almost helpless to do anything about it—unless they know the power of God. Grief over the loss of children is in the same class as the loss of labor and income. This is not a blessing—it's a curse.

The Wealth of Solomon

The book of Proverbs says more about wealth and riches than any other book in the Bible. Why? Because no one has ever surpassed Solomon in real goods. He was the wealthiest man who ever lived.

Let's see what Solomon said concerning prosperity. Proverbs 6:6-11:

Go to the ant, thou sluggard; consider her ways, and be wise: Which having no guide, overseer, or ruler, provideth her meat in the summer, and gathereth her food in the harvest. How long wilt thou sleep, O sluggard? when wilt thou arise out of thy sleep?

Yet a little sleep, a little slumber, a little folding of the hands to sleep: So shall thy poverty come as one that travelleth, and thy want as an armed man.

Notice that Solomon used the ant as an example. Are ants poverty stricken? No! They are hard workers. The more you put into something, the more you will get out of it.

Also, pay attention to how Solomon refers to poverty as a traveling, armed robber. Who is another robber the Bible says goes about as a roaring lion seeking whom he may devour? *The devil.* That roar is his arm—his weapon.

In the past, Satan has made us back off from him because his roar convinced us that he could really bite. But that's not true. Jesus pulled his teeth! The Captain of our salvation disarmed the adversary through His substitutionary sacrifice at Calvary. Thank God, Jesus took his armor away from him and then armed the Body of Christ from head to toe so that *we* could stop the devil.

Poverty destroys. It goes around like an armed robber. God calls lack a curse, so there is no way it could ever be a blessing.

Jesus came to minister to the poor. Why? To make them poorer? Of course not! The Bible says He became poor that we might become rich (2 Corinthians 8:9). He bore the curse of poverty in order to get us out of it—not to leave us in it.

The Blessing of Abraham

"Christ hath redeemed us from the curse of the law, being made a curse for us: for it is written, Cursed is everyone that hangeth on a tree: That the blessing of Abraham might come on the Gentiles through Jesus Christ; that we might receive the promise of the Spirit through faith" (Galatians 3:13-14).

Remember, God has given us a choice. Let's go back to Deuteronomy 28 and see what a blessing is, so that we will know what to choose.

Verses 1-2 say, "And it shall come to pass, if thou shalt hearken diligently unto the voice of the Lord thy God, to observe and to do all his commandments which I command thee this day, that the Lord thy God will set thee on high above all nations of the earth: And all these blessings shall come on thee, and overtake thee…."

Look at verse 4: "Blessed shall be the fruit of thy body, and the fruit of thy ground, and the fruit of thy cattle, the increase of thy kine, and the flocks of thy sheep." Obviously, increase is a blessing.

Verse 8: "The Lord shall command the blessing upon thee in thy storehouses, and in all that thou settest thine hand unto; and he shall bless thee in the land which the Lord thy God giveth thee." God wants to increase His people. Psalm 35:27 says that He has *pleasure* in the prosperity of His servants.

Why Does God Prosper Us?

Now that we have established the fact that prosperity is a blessing, we must know why God wants us to flourish in the financial realm.

Genesis 39:2-3 says that the Lord was with Joseph and that God made all he did to prosper. The New Testament application is Philippians 4:19. It says that the Father will meet our needs according to His riches in glory.

Why is God going to be with us and cause all that we do to prosper? Deuteronomy 8:18 has the answer. "But thou shalt remember the Lord thy God: for it is he that giveth thee power to get wealth, that he may establish his covenant which he sware unto thy fathers, as it is this day." The power to get wealth comes from God. He gives it in order to establish His covenant.

The purpose for abundance is to preach the gospel, feed the poor and meet the needs of others.

Proverbs 28:8 says, "He that by usury and unjust gain increaseth his substance, he shall gather it for him that will pity the poor." That's for us, the Body of Christ! We should be able to get together and buy a load of grain and feed a multitude with it. That's the reason for wealth and prosperity.

God increases us so that we can increase our production in the Word. That's what we are here for—to establish God's covenant. God doesn't prosper us financially just so that we can be more comfortable. He doesn't heal us so we can watch television without pain in our bodies.

Wealth is not to provide more conveniences and luxuries. Without the Word directing our lives, that's exactly what will happen. This has been a major problem in the Body of Christ as prosperity has been preached. A great number of people in the Body use the increase of God just to become more comfortable. I've been guilty of it myself, but thank God I've repented. I believe the Body of Christ is beginning to wake up. We're beginning to use our increase to win the world instead of increasing our own goods. God wants you to prosper, not just to put food on your table, but also to reach out and help provide food for someone else. Prosperity enables you to be about your Father's business— meeting the needs of others, spirit, soul and body.

If you give, it will be given to you. As you seek first the kingdom of God—to reach out to others as Jesus reached out—God will supernaturally meet your needs.

Change your image today. Begin seeing yourself as the one giving to supply the needs of mankind. A prosperous man is one who helps to establish God's covenant and understands that his needs will be taken care of. He takes his eyes off of himself and looks to the needs of others. His reason for working is to have so that he can give to those who are in need (Ephesians 4:28).

Prosperity is a blessing for the world. Walk in that revelation today! You are a giver. Choose life and blessing, and see the miraculous take place right in your own home!

4

The Fool's Dozen

Christians have avoided prosperity like the plague because they have been taught that it would defile them. But prosperity will only result in destruction when the one who seeks it is without the fear of the Lord and without the wisdom of God.

Notice Proverbs 1:28-32:

Then shall they call upon me [wisdom], but I will not answer; they shall seek me early, but they shall not find me: for that they hated knowledge, and did not choose the fear of the Lord: They would none of my counsel: they despised all my reproof. Therefore shall they eat of the fruit of their own way, and be filled with their own devices. For the turning away of the

simple shall slay them, and *the prosperity
of fools shall destroy them.*

Psalm 73:12 tells us that the ungodly prosper
in the world by increasing in riches. Whether
financial success will destroy us or not has to do
with whether we are thriving in the world or in
the Word.

A man may accumulate a great deal of money
and still not be prosperous. Wealth without a personal knowledge of God can cause him to have
ulcers! The Scripture promises that if we will exalt
the Word of God, its wisdom will promote us
(Proverbs 4:8). That's the difference between prospering in the world and prospering in the Word.

The Bible says that prosperity ruins the fool.
Therefore, the spiritual laws of abundance warrant
that we avoid the things which are foolishness in
God's sight.

These things are what I call the "Fool's Dozen."

God's Definition of a Fool

1. A fool despises wisdom and instruction
(Proverbs 1:7). He won't obey the Word. He
despises godly wisdom.

2. A fool is right in his own eyes (Proverbs 12:15). He thinks that his way is always right. He cannot be corrected.

3. A fool makes a mockery of sin (Proverbs 14:9). This is the Christian who thinks it's all right to watch R-rated or X-rated movies. He figures they really won't hurt him. Prosperity will eventually bring ruin because he will end up spending God's money on that trash. God is not mocked—this man will reap what he sows.

This is the person who feels he can serve Jesus and still drink "just a tiny bit." "It won't hurt, it's only a little." He is making a mockery of sin. The human liver was not made to process alcohol. The wages of sin is death. This person is wasting money on something that is bringing destruction. Wealth will destroy him.

4. A fool hides hatred by lying and slander (Proverbs 10:18). He talks ugly about people who have money, or he's angry with the government because he feels cheated.

No one has the right to slander the president or anyone else. We have the right and privilege to vote, then to intercede for those who are in the offices of our government.

5. A fool does mischief for sport (Proverbs 10:23). He vandalizes other people's property as a joke.

When I started driving, my dad used to tell me, "Now, boy, you don't have to screech those rear tires every time you leave a signal light! One of these days you'll have to buy your own tires and you'll quit that!" He was right!

The first time I had to spend $100 on a set of tires they almost had to peel the bills out of my hand. I had never even seen that much money in one place at one time and it was just like Dad said—it cured me. I stopped tearing things up just for sport when it started costing me.

6. A fool has a perverted mouth. "Better is the poor that walketh in his integrity, than he that is perverse in his lips, and is a fool" (Proverbs 19:1). A perverted mouth is manifest several ways. The obvious way is profanity, but perverse lips can also mean disobedient speech—saying things that oppose the Word of God.

Another form of a perverted mouth is exaggeration. When a fool sees a little dog, he calls it a big one. When he sees a big dog, he says it's small. He's always exaggerating.

When he wants to act on Mark 11:23 and have what he says, he can't—he has already deceived himself. His heart doesn't know what he means and what he doesn't mean. Angels and devils don't care whether he's sincere or not. They just hear and respond to his words.

Don't misunderstand me, you shouldn't be in bondage to your words. But I am talking about those who are never serious. You can never get a right answer out of them. They are always foolishly jesting.

Believers don't need those cute little things to sell themselves socially. We have the Spirit of God, faith and a godly personality inside us. That's enough to put us over.

7. *A fool trusts his own understanding* (Proverbs 28:26). The Word of God tells us not to rely on our own insight, but to trust in the Lord with all of our hearts. When we do, our prosperity will not bring ruin because God is directing our paths (Proverbs 3:5-6, *The Amplified Bible*).

8. *A fool utters all of his mind* (Proverbs 29:11). This is the person who says, "Bless God, I'm going to give them a piece of my mind." Nobody needs a share in that mess! It doesn't do

any good anyway, it only alienates.

This could also be the one who can't keep his mouth shut concerning spiritual things. Once the Holy Spirit begins to give him revelations and supernatural discerning, he blabs everything he knows. If God can't trust him with information, He can't trust him with wealth either.

9. *A fool walks in darkness* (Ecclesiastes 2:14). The Bible tells us to walk in the light. If we refuse to do it, we qualify as a fool and prosperity may destroy us. If we are walking in the dark, we may not know what to do with the abundance when it comes.

The next two points are related:

10. *A fool does not pay his vows* and 11. *God takes no pleasure in fools* (Ecclesiastes 5:4). You cannot imagine how many people have made faith promises to this ministry and have never followed through. If their motive for making financial pledges is to put God in a corner and obligate Him to a hundredfold return on their giving, then they are out of line. That's foolish to begin with, but to make a pledge and not pay it makes a person a fool in God's eyes.

If I were making a pledge and something

came up that kept me from fulfilling my promise to a ministry, I'd at least give a portion of it. Then I'd write and tell them that I'll not give up, praise God. I'll not quit, and when I have it, I'll send it. I would then encourage that ministry with my faith and prayers. So many don't even do that, much less come up with what they have pledged.

12. God takes pleasure in the prosperity of His servants, but He receives no enjoyment from the foolish. The book of Hebrews tells us that Jehovah was not pleased with the children of Israel because they failed in the wilderness. The same is true today. He is not pleased with us when we fail to keep our vows.

We don't receive offerings into this ministry just so that we can get something. We receive them so that fruit may abound to your account. You cannot give without receiving a return. Giving sets a law into motion. God uses your giving to bless you.

13. A fool is swallowed up by his own lips (Ecclesiastes 10:12). This is the man who is snared by his own words. He has no control over his mouth.

14. A fool says in his heart, "There is no God"

(Psalm 14:1). Someone might say, "Wait a minute, Brother Copeland, I've always believed in God. I'm born again and filled with the Holy Spirit." Though that same person might never speak it with his mouth, he may say it in his heart through his actions. He's like the one who thinks it's all right to watch an immoral movie or read a little pornographic trash. He is saying in his heart, *There is no God.* He doesn't think that he will reap what he *sows.*

This is when the devil is most insidious. Satan doesn't care whether we publicly proclaim to be an atheist or whether we are a fool as a believer, just so long as he can trap us.

Psalm 53:1 links it with corruption. "The fool hath said in his heart, There is no God. Corrupt are they...." Destruction will be the result, whether we believe it or not. These are laws and we can't cross them without a certain amount of financial decline being the result.

15. A fool is slow to believe in his heart (Luke 24:25). This last area spawns from the previous one. If a fellow hasn't given a part of his life to God, it is the same as saying in his heart that God doesn't exist. He is slow to believe and trust God

with that aspect of his life. The Father can't afford
to prosper this poor fellow because he will do
more harm than good.

Spiritual and Physical Laws

We must understand that there are laws
governing everything in existence. Nothing is by
accident. There are laws in the world of the spirit,
and laws in the world of the natural. The laws
of the natural realm govern the natural, physical
world and our activities in it. If the law of gravity
were not in effect, for example, we would float in
the air.

We need to realize that the laws of the spiritual world are more powerful than the laws of the
physical world. Spiritual law gave birth to physical
law. The world and the physical forces governing
it were created by the power of faith—a spiritual
force. God, a Spirit, created all matter with the
force of faith. Hebrews 11:3 says, "...the worlds
were framed by the word of God, so that things
which are seen were not made of things which do
appear." The law of gravity would be meaningless if
it were not a real force. The force of gravity makes

the law of gravity work. Faith is a spiritual force, a spiritual energy, a spiritual power. The force of faith makes the laws of the spirit world function.

Two Spiritual Laws

Romans 8:2 says, "For the law of the Spirit of life in Christ Jesus hath made me free from the law of sin and death." There are two functional laws in the world of the spirit. One, the law of sin and death, was set in motion by Adam when he disobeyed God in the Garden of Eden. The other, the law of the Spirit of life, was put into operation by Jesus Christ at His resurrection. The law of the Spirit of life is the master law under which we operate as children of God. It supersedes the law of sin and death, and faith causes it to function. Salvation is available to every human being on the face of the earth because the Word says that anyone who calls on the Name of the Lord shall be saved (Joel 2:32; Romans 10:13). But this higher spiritual law of life will only work when it is put to work.

This same rule is true in prosperity. There are certain laws governing prosperity that are revealed in God's Word. Faith causes them to function. They will work when they are put to work, and they will stop when the force of faith is stopped.

The Bible says that God's Word is established forever (1 Peter 1:25). When God speaks, His words become law in the world of the spirit. Jesus said, "Man shall not live by bread alone, but by every word that proceedeth out of the mouth of God" (Matthew 4:4).

Results

The success formulas in the Word of God produce results when used as directed. Mark 11:23 says, "…whosoever shall say unto this mountain, Be thou removed, and be thou cast into the sea; and shall not doubt in his heart, but shall believe that those things which he saith shall come to pass; he shall have whatsoever he saith." Here, Jesus introduced a principle—a spiritual law—that works. It doesn't make sense to the natural mind that with faith you can have what-ever you say, though it may be contrary to what you can see with your physical eye. But Jesus said it, and by the eternal Almighty God, *it is so!* When you act on it, mix your faith with it and don't doubt in your heart, this spiritual law will work for you!

Take the following scriptures and *meditate* on them. Develop a true image of you and your family prospering based on what the Word of God says about you. *Believe* it in your heart.

Then *speak* these scriptures out loud! Put these spiritual laws to work. Claim them as your own. See yourself giving to the needs of those around you. Remember, meeting the needs of others with God's power is what prosperity is all about.

Let them shout for joy, and be glad, that favour my righteous cause: yea, let them say continually, Let the Lord be magnified, which hath pleasure in the prosperity of his servant. And my tongue shall speak of thy righteousness and of thy praise all the day long (Psalm 35:27-28).

Give, and it shall be given unto you; good measure, pressed down, and shaken together, and running over, shall men give into your bosom. For with the same measure that ye mete withal it shall be measured to you again (Luke 6:38).

Therefore take no thought, saying, What shall we eat? or, What shall we drink? or, Wherewithal shall we be clothed? (For after all these things do the Gentiles seek:) for your heavenly Father knoweth that ye have need of all these things. But seek ye first the kingdom of God, and his right-eousness; and all these things shall be added unto you (Matthew 6:31-33).

Prayer for Salvation and Baptism in the Holy Spirit

Heavenly Father, I come to You in the Name of Jesus. Your Word says, "Whosoever shall call on the name of the Lord shall be saved" (Acts 2:21). I am calling on You. I pray and ask Jesus to come into my heart and be Lord over my life according to Romans 10:9-10: "If thou shalt confess with thy mouth the Lord Jesus, and shalt believe in thine heart that God hath raised him from the dead, thou shalt be saved. For with the heart man believeth unto righteousness; and with the mouth confession is made unto salvation." I do that now. I confess that Jesus is Lord, and I believe in my heart that God raised Him from the dead.

I am now reborn! I am a Christian—a child of Almighty God! I am saved! You also said in Your Word, "If ye then, being evil, know how to give good gifts unto your children: HOW MUCH MORE shall your heavenly Father give the Holy Spirit to them that ask him?" (Luke 11:13). I'm also asking You to fill me with the Holy Spirit. Holy Spirit, rise up within me as I praise God. I fully expect to speak with other tongues as You give me the utterance (Acts 2:4). In Jesus' Name. Amen!

Begin to praise God for filling you with the Holy Spirit. Speak those words and syllables you receive—not in your own language, but the language given to you by the Holy Spirit. You have to use your own voice. God will not force you to speak. Don't be concerned with how it sounds. It is a heavenly language!

Continue with the blessing God has given you and pray in the spirit every day.

You are a born-again, Spirit-filled believer. You'll never be the same!

Find a good church that boldly preaches God's Word and obeys it. Become a part of a church family who will love and care for you as you love and care for them.

We need to be connected to each other. It increases our strength in God. It's God's plan for us.

Make it a habit to watch the *Believer's Voice of Victory* television broadcast and become a doer of the Word, who is blessed in his doing (James 1:22-25).

About the Author

Kenneth Copeland is co-founder and president of Kenneth Copeland Ministries in Fort Worth, Texas, and best-selling author of books that include *How to Discipline Your Flesh* and *Honor—Walking in Honesty, Truth and Integrity.*

Now in his 40th year as a minister of the gospel of Christ and teacher of God's Word, Kenneth is the recording artist of such award-winning albums as his Grammy-nominated *Only the Redeemed, In His Presence, He Is Jehovah, Just a Closer Walk* and his most recently released *Big Band Gospel* album. He also co-stars as the character Wichita Slim in the children's adventure videos *The Gunslinger, Covenant Rider* and the movie *The Treasure of Eagle Mountain,* and as Daniel Lyon in the *Commander Kellie and the Superkids*$_{SM}$ videos *Armor of Light* and *Judgment: The Trial of Commander Kellie.*

With the help of offices and staff in the United States, Canada, England, Australia, South Africa and Ukraine, Kenneth is fulfilling his vision to boldly preach the uncompromised Word of God from the top of this world, to the bottom, and all the way around. His ministry reaches millions of people worldwide through daily and Sunday TV broadcasts, magazines, teaching audios and videos, conventions and campaigns, and the World Wide Web.

Learn more about Kenneth Copeland Ministries by visiting our Web site at www.kcm.org

Books Available From
Kenneth Copeland Ministries

by Kenneth Copeland

*   A Ceremony of Marriage

    A Matter of Choice

    Covenant of Blood

    Faith and Patience—The Power Twins

*   Freedom From Fear

    Giving and Receiving

    Honor—Walking in Honesty, Truth and Integrity

    How to Conquer Strife

    How to Discipline Your Flesh

    How to Receive Communion

    In Love There Is No Fear

    Know Your Enemy

    Living at the End of Time—A Time of
        Supernatural Increase

    Love Never Fails

*   Mercy—The Divine Rescue of the Human Race

*   Now Are We in Christ Jesus

    One Nation Under God (gift book with CD enclosed)

*   Our Covenant With God

    Partnership—Sharing the Vision, Sharing the Grace

*   Prayer—Your Foundation for Success

*   Prosperity: The Choice Is Yours

    Rumors of War

*   Sensitivity of Heart

*   Six Steps to Excellence in Ministry

*   Sorrow Not! Winning Over Grief and Sorrow

*   The Decision Is Yours

*   The Force of Faith

by Gloria Copeland

*Available in Spanish

Living in Heaven's Blessings Now

Looking for a Receiver

*   Love—The Secret to Your Success

No Deposit—No Return

Pleasing the Father

Pressing In—It's Worth It All

Shine On!

The Grace That Makes Us Holy

The Power to Live a New Life

The Protection of Angels

There Is No High Like the Most High

The Secret Place of God's Protection (gift book with CD enclosed)

The Unbeatable Spirit of Faith

This Same Jesus

To Know Him

True Prosperity

Walk With God

Well Worth the Wait

Words That Heal (gift book with CD enclosed)

Your Promise of Protection—The Power of the 91st Psalm

Books Co-Authored by Kenneth and Gloria Copeland

Family Promises

Healing Promises

Prosperity Promises

Protection Promises

*   From Faith to Faith—A Daily Guide to Victory

From Faith to Faith—A Perpetual Calendar

One Word From God Can Change Your Life

One Word From God Series:

- One Word From God Can Change Your Destiny
- One Word From God Can Change Your Family
- One Word From God Can Change Your Finances
- One Word From God Can Change Your Formula for Success
- One Word From God Can Change Your Health
- One Word From God Can Change Your Nation
- One Word From God Can Change Your Prayer Life
- One Word From God Can Change Your Relationships

Load Up—A Youth Devotional
Over the Edge—A Youth Devotional
Pursuit of His Presence—A Daily Devotional
Pursuit of His Presence—A Perpetual Calendar
Raising Children Without Fear

Other Books Published by KCP

Real People. Real Needs. Real Victories.
    A book of testimonies to encourage your faith
John G. Lake—His Life, His Sermons, His
    Boldness of Faith
The Holiest of All by Andrew Murray
The New Testament in Modern Speech by
    Richard Francis Weymouth
The Rabbi From Burbank by Isidor Zwirn and Bob Owen
Unchained! by Mac Gober

Products Designed for Today's Children and Youth

And Jesus Healed Them All (confession book and CD gift package)
Baby Praise Board Book
Baby Praise Christmas Board Book

*Available in Spanish

Noah's Ark Coloring Book

The Best of *Shout!* Adventure Comics

The *Shout!* Giant Flip Coloring Book

The *Shout!* Joke Book

The *Shout!* Super-Activity Book

Wichita Slim's Campfire Stories

*Commander Kellie and the Superkids*_{SM} Books:

The SWORD Adventure Book

*Commander Kellie and the Superkids*_{SM} Solve-It-Yourself Mysteries

*Commander Kellie and the Superkids*_{SM} Adventure Series:

Middle Grade Novels by Christopher P.N. Maselli:

#1   The Mysterious Presence

#2   The Quest for the Second Half

#3   Escape From Jungle Island

#4   In Pursuit of the Enemy

#5   Caged Rivalry

#6   Mystery of the Missing Junk

#7   Out of Breath

#8   The Year Mashela Stole Christmas

#9   False Identity

#10 The Runaway Mission

#11 The Knight-Time Rescue of Commander Kellie

World Offices
Kenneth Copeland Ministries

For more information about KCM and our products,
please write to the office nearest you:

Kenneth Copeland Ministries
Fort Worth, TX 76192-0001

Kenneth Copeland
Locked Bag 2600
Mansfield Delivery Centre
QUEENSLAND 4122
AUSTRALIA

Kenneth Copeland
Post Office Box 15
BATH
BA1 3XN
U.K.

Kenneth Copeland
Private Bag X 909
FONTAINEBLEAU
2032
REPUBLIC OF
SOUTH AFRICA

Kenneth Copeland
PO Box 3111 STN LCD 1
Langley BC V3A 4R3
CANADA

Kenneth Copeland Ministries
Post Office Box 84
L'VIV 79000
UKRAINE

We're Here for You!

Believer's Voice of Victory Television Broadcast

Join Kenneth and Gloria Copeland and the *Believer's Voice of Victory* broadcasts Monday through Friday and on Sunday each week, and learn how faith in God's Word can take your life from ordinary to extraordinary. This teaching from God's Word is designed to get you where you want to be—*on top!*

You can catch the *Believer's Voice of Victory* broadcast on your local, cable or satellite channels.* Also available 24 hours on webcast at BVOV.TV.

* Check your local listings for times and stations in your area.

Believer's Voice of Victory Magazine

Enjoy inspired teaching and encouragement from Kenneth and Gloria Copeland and guest ministers each month in the *Believer's Voice of Victory* magazine. Also included are real-life testimonies of God's miraculous power and divine intervention in the lives of people just like you!

It's more than just a magazine—it's a ministry.

To receive a FREE subscription to *Believer's Voice of Victory,* write to:

Kenneth Copeland Ministries
Fort Worth, TX 76192-0001
Or call:
800-600-7395
(7 a.m.-5 p.m. CT)
Or visit our Web site at:
www.kcm.org

If you are writing from outside the U.S., please contact the KCM office nearest you. Addresses for all Kenneth Copeland Ministries offices are listed on the previous pages.